Neo Leo

The Ageless Ideas of Leonardo da Vinci

GENE BARRETTA

SCHOLASTIC INC.
New York   Toronto   London   Auckland
Sydney   New Delhi   Hong Kong

Leonardo da Vinci was fascinated by the world around him. He studied animals and people. He watched plants grow and birds fly. He explored the mighty rivers. Nature was his teacher. It inspired his remarkable studies and inventions.

Leonardo's ideas were revolutionary. But they remained buried among his 20,000 pages of notes. Most of his inventions were not built during his lifetime. The designs were either too expensive, too sophisticated, or too controversial.

Sadly, most of his ideas have been lost to time. But the surviving notes prove that he was a true visionary.

For example . . .

Neo 1903
The Wright Brothers are famous for creating an engine-powered aircraft that could carry a person into the sky.

Leo

Person can stand or lie down to operate it.

Wings bend at the center like a bird.

Four hundred years earlier, Leonardo had designed several man-powered aircraft, including the ornithopter. He wanted to give people the ability to fly like the birds he passionately studied.

Neo 1891

Otto Lilienthal had actually seen Leonardo's
ornithopter drawings in the late 1880s.
He was motivated to develop history's
first successful hang glider.

Leonardo designed his glider after watching leaves glide through the air.

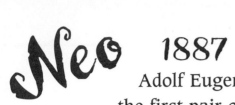

1887

Adolf Eugen Fick is responsible for making and fitting the first pair of successful contact lenses.

Oddly enough, he tested them on animals.

→

1895

Thomas Edison's Kinetoscope was the forerunner of the modern movie projector . . .

→

Leo Leonardo's diagrams show detailed concepts of a contact lens. He used light and water to conduct advanced studies in vision and magnification.

. . . but it was not the first example of a projector. Leonardo figured out how to use light to project images through a lens.

Neo **1781**

Thomas Paine exhibited a model of his single-span bridge in Benjamin Franklin's garden. At the time, no one believed his bridge could work, especially without the usual support piers to hold up the center.

Leo

Leonardo believed that a single-span bridge was surely possible. But like Mr. Paine, he never saw his bridge constructed. He also proved the value of truss bridges. Leonardo's experiments confirmed that a triangular truss would resist tension better than the older box structures. He proposed a two-level truss bridge—the bottom level for transportation and the top level for pedestrians.

Triangular truss support

Top view

No support piers in the center

Pedestrian level

Transportation level

Neo 1916

The world had not seen a tank in action until World War I. The British Navy developed it, and Captain H. W. Mortimore brought one into battle for the first time.

Leo

Leonardo was thinking about tanks long before Captain Mortimore. Turtles became his model. He considered himself a pacifist but looked at weapons as a design challenge. He also designed grenades, machine guns, and a giant catapult, among others.

Neo

1870

James Starley is credited as the father of the British bicycle industry. Many of his inventions led us closer to the type of bicycles we ride today.

Leo

A design for
a chain link

Drawing is too
amateurish
for Leonardo

Gears with squared teeth
do not work. Later, he
rounded them to make
the chain function.

Did Leonardo invent the bicycle?

A bicycle does appear in Leonardo's notes. While historians agree that it is not his drawing, some think that a pupil drew it after studying a bicycle prototype in Leonardo's workshop. Others say it was drawn as a prank by someone centuries later.

We may never know for sure, although we do know that Leonardo had designed many parts that are used to build bicycles, such as gears and chains.

Neo 1907

Paul Cornu was a bicycle maker by trade. He built the very first helicopter to lift off vertically. It hovered one foot above the ground for twenty seconds.

Four men operate it.

Wings turn like a screw.

Air compresses under wing.

Prior to that, Leonardo devised his own version of the helicopter—the helical screw. It used the same principle as modern helicopters for compressing air to achieve liftoff.

Unfortunately, the weight of his machine and the man-powered mechanics would have prevented real flight.

Neo Modern boats have fish-shaped hulls, unlike the square-shaped hulls of days gone by. And all passenger ships today are required to have double hulls for extra protection.

→

1943

Jacques Cousteau and Emile Gagnan made modern diving equipment popular when they designed underwater breathing equipment called the Aqua-Lung.

→

Leo

Long before these features were accepted, Leonardo watched fish swim and realized that their body shapes were ideal for traveling through water.

He also envisioned a double-hull body to keep boats afloat after being rammed.

Scuba gear existed much earlier than Leonardo. But he added his own features, such as an inflatable bag to raise and lower a diver and a reinforced breathing tube.

Neo With the use of modern imaging technology, doctors now understand that when blood moves through the heart, it forms a vortex that opens and closes the valves.

Leo

Leonardo had already figured it out. Through detailed body dissection and simulated water experiments, he discovered and diagrammed accurate examples of vortex formation in the blood.

Neo What do a steam locomotive and a cooking rotisserie have in common? Leonardo da Vinci, of course.

Leo

His notebooks are filled with experiments on steam power and air pressure, predicting the development of the steam engine. He understood that hot air rises and used that knowledge to operate an automatic rotisserie. The first!

Steam expands and forces the lid to rise.

Heated water makes steam.

Hot air rises and turns a fan.

The fan turns the rotisserie.

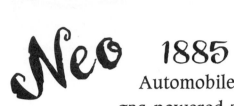

1885

Automobile engineer Karl Benz invented the first gas-powered automobile and essentially launched the auto industry.

1940

When people attended the 1940 World's Fair in New York they came face-to-face with Elektro and Sparko, two of the world's earliest robots.

Leo

Leonardo's self-propelled cart foreshadowed both the automobile and the robot. The cart was spring-powered. Levers and gears were used to program its movements like a primitive robot.

Leonardo designed and actually constructed robots for royalty and court pageants. Springs, levers, water, and weights powered and controlled them.

Steering system

Coil springs beneath toothed gears

Pedals controlled steering system.

Regulated the timing of springs

Could sit and stand

Lion's chest opened and flowers spilled out.

Wheels underneath

Steering device

Neo 1785

Jean-Pierre Blanchard created the original all-fabric parachute and was the first to prove that it could provide safe escape from a hot-air balloon. Actually, his dog proved it.

Leo

Or one could argue that Leonardo proved it before both of them. He had a different purpose for his parachute. Its function was for traveling from high to low surfaces like the birds he observed. His triangle design, unfortunately, was never tested . . .

Closely woven linen

24 feet squared by 24 feet high

Air pressure helps the parachute float.

. . . until now!

That's right. Leonardo's ideas are finally coming to life. Several are being built and tested. And they are working!

Adrian Nicholas built and flew Leonardo's parachute.

Vebjørn Sand's team built the single-span bridge.

Mark Rosheim built and operated the self-propelled cart and robot knight.

Dr. Mory Gharib built and confirmed the success of Leonardo's artificial heart valve model.

Steve Roberts and Martin Kimm built Leonardo's glider. Judy Leden flew it.

The amount of knowledge and vision found in Leonardo's notes is overwhelming. And remember—about two-thirds of his notes are still missing! Imagine what is left to learn from this incredible inventor.

Bibliography

BOOKS

Cooper, Margaret. *The Inventions of Leonardo da Vinci*. New York: Macmillan, 1965.

Laurenza, Domenico. *Leonardo's Machines: Da Vinci's Inventions Revealed*. Edited by Mario Taddei and Edoardo Zanon. Cincinnati: A David & Charles Book, 2006.

Reti, Ladislao, ed. *The Unknown Leonardo*. New York: McGraw Hill, 1974.

Websites

The Leonardo Museum in Vinci. www.museoleonardiano.it/eng

National Museum of Science and Technology: Leonardo Da Vinci. www.museoscienza.org/english.

Universal Leonardo. www.universalleonardo.org.

DVDS

Leonardo's Dream Machines. PBS Home Video, 2005.

The Life of Leonardo da Vinci: The Most Brilliant Mind in History. Chicago: 2003.

Modern Marvels: Da Vinci Tech. The History Channel, 2005.

To Nella and Bruce Storm,
for making the Renaissance
come alive for a ten-year-old.
Most boys wanted to be astronauts
or firemen; I wanted to be Leonardo.

Love, your dear boy
—G. B.

Watercolor on Arches cold-press paper was used to create the illustrations for this book.
Designed by April Ward.

Copyright © 2009 by Gene Barretta.
All rights reserved. Published by Scholastic Inc., 557 Broadway, New York, NY 10012, by arrangement with Henry Holt and Company, LLC.
Printed in the U.S.A.

ISBN-13: 978-0-545-62240-0
ISBN-10: 0-545-62240-9

7 8 9 10   40   22 21 20 19 18 17 16